# J.M. HAWTHORNE

# Freedom From Identity Politics

*Keep Being Yourself While Thinking For Yourself*

Copyright © 2024 by J.M. Hawthorne

All rights reserved. No part of this publication may be reproduced, stored or transmitted in any form or by any means, electronic, mechanical, photocopying, recording, scanning, or otherwise without written permission from the publisher. It is illegal to copy this book, post it to a website, or distribute it by any other means without permission.

J.M. Hawthorne asserts the moral right to be identified as the author of this work.

J.M. Hawthorne has no responsibility for the persistence or accuracy of URLs for external or third-party Internet Websites referred to in this publication and does not guarantee that any content on such Websites is, or will remain, accurate or appropriate.

Designations used by companies to distinguish their products are often claimed as trademarks. All brand names and product names used in this book and on its cover are trade names, service marks, trademarks and registered trademarks of their respective owners. The publishers and the book are not associated with any product or vendor mentioned in this book. None of the companies referenced within the book have endorsed the book.

First edition

This book was professionally typeset on Reedsy.
Find out more at reedsy.com

"Everyone is in favor of free speech.
Hardly a day passes without it being
extolled, but some people's idea of it
is that they are free to say what they
like, but if anyone says anything back,
that is an outrage."

-WINSTON CHURCHILL

# Contents

# Introduction

I was inspired to write this book during my journey to becoming a political independent. I grew up as a dedicated liberal and became deeply interested in politics around the age of 17, during the Bush v. Gore election in 2000. Although I missed the chance to vote that year due to my December birthday, the controversy over hanging chads and ballot issues in Florida dominated my American Democracy class and ignited my political curiosity.

Even though many of my views aligned with the Democrats at the time, I was always eager to seek more information and understand the underlying reasons. I loved debating and listening to different perspectives. My grandfather, a WWII veteran and passionate patriot, often engaged me in thoughtful political discussions, emphasizing the importance of understanding diverse viewpoints, which I believe is a cornerstone of our nation's greatness.

The events of 9/11 further fueled my quest for understanding. As a freshman in college in September 2001, I was driven to comprehend the motivations behind such an attack. This led me to enroll in a course titled "Islamic Politics" in the spring of 2002, despite being a business student surrounded by history majors. My classmates often questioned my presence in the course, but my curiosity about the roots of jihad and the true nature of Islam was insatiable. Although I may not have found all the answers I sought, this experience underscored the importance of exploring different perspectives.

By 2008, my political stance had shifted to a more centrist and populist view. Having graduated college, met my future wife, and become an ardent supporter of Barack Obama, I was inspired by his message of hope and positivity during uncertain economic times. I became politically active, volunteering for the campaign, knocking on doors, and making phone calls. My grandfather frequently quoted political figures, with one of his favorites being JFK's famous line: "Ask not what your country can do for you, but what you can do for your country."

From 2011 through about 2014, I began to question some of the further left leaning things coming through the Obama Administration, despite his centrist and populist messages. This time my questioning and curiosity as to "why" led me down what others may call a "conspiracy theory rabbit hole", learning about concepts like the New World Order, 9/11 theories, etc. Debates on the validity of these theories we can leave for another book or discussion.

Throughout these experiences, my commitment to understanding diverse viewpoints and my passion for political engagement have only grown stronger, shaping my path as a political independent.

Ahead to 2016, I was one of many Americans who voted for Obama, and then moved to the anti-establishment vote of Donald Trump. Trump represented to me, like Obama, a Populist, America first message. As a political independent, voting for Hillary Clinton was not an option for me.

The vitriol and hatred that emerged from the election and continued in the years that followed between the far left and far right made independents and centrists like me cringe.

I began to ask questions like:

- "Can we communicate without yelling at one another?"
- "Why is everyone so triggered by things?"
- "Why can't a person from both sides have a discussion of understanding like my grandfather and I used to have?"
- "Why are people labeling whole groups of people as racists, socialists, snowflakes, neocons, libtards, fascists, and many others?"

## *This was the tipping point*

I wanted so desperately to have conversations with people and try to understand. While social media is not the best place to have discussions of substance with people, I still tried. With my grandfather having since passed away, I sought out anyone who would listen to engage in these dialogues.

I commented on a Facebook friend's post in 2017, supporting a decision or vote made by Trump. It wasn't a controversial comment, but someone I didn't know replied, calling me a racist.

There was nothing racial in the entire thread. Then it dawned on me: he labeled me a "racist" simply because I am a white male who voted for Trump.

This is when I first learned about Identity Politics. This was an example of one of the stereotypical negatives of Identity Politics: assuming that because of my race and background that I must be a racist, or I must believe in this, or support that. I felt like my independent thought was lost, that I had no voice, no chance of just a friendly or thoughtful discussion.

As I had done so many times in the past, I was curious. What is identity Politics? Can it be good? Is it bad? Where do we go from here? Can we get back to a place where two people can sit down like my grandfather and me, and just have a discussion?

Join me as we explore this topic. We will start by defining Identity politics and looking at historical references for context. Then we will explore different viewpoints to uncover the pros and cons of identity politics. Through the pros and cons of Identity Politics, I hope there is a future where Americans can have independent thought, while maintaining their identity and connection with their communities.

# Part 1 - Defining Identity Politics

Let's begin by defining Identity Politics.

**Here are a few definitions:**

1. *Merriam-Webster defines identity politics as* "politics in which groups of people having a particular racial, religious, ethnic, social, or cultural identity tend to promote their own specific interests or concerns without regard to the interests or concerns of any larger political group."
2. *The Stanford Encyclopedia of Philosophy describes identity politics as* "a wide range of political activity and theorizing founded in the shared experiences of injustice of members of certain social groups."
3. *Oxford Reference states that identity politics* "is a term that refers to political positions based on the interests and perspectives of social groups with which people identify."

These published definitions can be jointly summarized as political positions or perspectives based on the interests and viewpoints of social groups with which individuals identify. These groups can include, but are not limited to, race, gender, sexuality, religion, and nationality. Identity politics is often used to advocate for the rights and interests of marginalized or disadvantaged groups, highlighting issues of systemic inequality and discrimination.

The term "identity politics" originated in the late 20th century, although the practice itself can be traced back to earlier periods. Its origins are most commonly associated with the civil rights movements of the 1960s and 1970s. These movements aimed to address systemic injustices and discrimination faced by various marginalized groups. For example, the civil rights movement sought to end racial segregation and discrimination against African Americans, while the feminist movement aimed to achieve gender equality, and the LGBTQ+ rights movement fought for the rights of sexual minorities.

The Combahee River Collective, a Black feminist lesbian organization, is often credited with coining the term "identity politics" in their 1977 statement. They emphasized that their identity as Black women shaped their political experiences and priorities, highlighting the importance of considering intersecting identities when addressing social issues (Taylor, 2017). This notion of intersectionality, later elaborated by scholar Kimberlé Crenshaw, underscores the interconnected nature of social categorizations and their cumulative impact on individuals and groups (Crenshaw, 1989).

Identity politics is grounded in the belief that individuals' social identities profoundly influence their political perspectives and experiences. These identities can include race, gender, sexuality, class, religion, disability, and more. The core principles of identity politics include:

1. **Recognition of Difference:** Identity politics acknowledges that different social groups experience distinct forms of oppression and privilege. By recognizing these differences, advocates can better address the specific needs and challenges faced by various groups.

2. **Empowerment of Marginalized Groups:** Identity politics seeks to empower marginalized groups by providing them with a platform to voice their concerns and advocate for their rights. This empowerment is seen as essential for achieving social justice and equality.

3. **Intersectionality:** Intersectionality is a key component of identity politics, emphasizing that individuals often belong to multiple social groups simultaneously. This means that their experiences of oppression or privilege are shaped by the intersection of these various identities.

4. **Political Mobilization:** Identity politics involves the mobilization of individuals around their shared identities to effect political change. This can take the form of grassroots organizing, advocacy, and lobbying efforts aimed at addressing specific social issues.

# Part 2- Pros and Cons of Identity Politics

Pros

While it is often seen through a polarizing lens, there are several positives associated with identity politics that contribute to social justice, representation, and inclusivity.

One of the most significant benefits of identity politics is its role in giving a voice to marginalized and underrepresented groups. Historically, many communities—such as racial minorities, women, LGBTQ+ individuals, and people with disabilities—have been excluded from political processes and decision-making. Identity politics brings their unique experiences and struggles to the forefront, ensuring that their specific needs and issues are addressed. This inclusion fosters a more equitable society where policies and laws are shaped by the diversity of its population.

Furthermore, proponents of identity politics feel it promotes social cohesion by fostering a sense of community and solidarity among individuals who share similar experiences of marginalization. This collective identity can empower individuals, helping them to overcome feelings of isolation and to mobilize for change.

Identity politics has made significant contributions to political discourse and social movements. Some of the key impacts and contributions of identity politics include:

1. **Advancement of Civil Rights:** Identity politics has played a crucial role in advancing civil rights for various marginalized groups. The civil rights movement, feminist movement, LGBTQ+ rights movement, and other identity-based movements have achieved significant legal and social victories, such as the Civil Rights Act of 1964, the legalization of same-sex marriage in the United States, and increased awareness of gender inequality and sexual harassment.

2. **Intersectional Analysis:** Identity politics has introduced the concept of intersectionality, which has become an essential analytical tool for understanding the complexities of social identities and their impact on individuals' experiences. This has led to more nuanced discussions of social justice and equity.

3. **Challenging Dominant Narratives**: Identity politics challenges dominant narratives that often marginalize or erase the experiences of certain groups. By centering the voices and perspectives of marginalized communities, identity politics seeks to create a more inclusive and equitable society.

Identity politics also plays a crucial role in expanding the scope of democracy. It ensures that diverse perspectives are included in political discourse, making democratic institutions more reflective of the society they serve. When political parties and leaders address the concerns of various identity groups, it leads to more informed and balanced policy making. This inclusivity can result in policies that better serve the population as a whole, as they are crafted with a broader understanding of the different needs and challenges faced by various communities.\

Moreover, identity politics encourages personal empowerment and self-awareness. By recognizing and embracing their identities, individuals can better understand their place in society and the forces that shape their lives. This awareness can inspire personal and collective action, leading to a more engaged and active citizenry. It also fosters empathy and understanding among different groups, as individuals learn about the diverse experiences and challenges faced by others.

# Cons

To fully and diversely understand identity politics, it is essential to approach the topic with an open mind and consider different perspectives. Let's explore some of the concerns associated with identity politics.

Identity politics has several notable drawbacks. It can foster division and fragmentation within society by emphasizing differences over commonalities, potentially leading to an "us versus them" mentality. This focus on specific group identities can undermine social cohesion and unity.

Additionally, identity politics may prioritize individual identities over shared values or broader societal goals. This can marginalize those outside specific identity groups and create competitive victimhood, where groups vie for recognition and resources, hindering collective progress.

Another significant issue is that identity politics can stifle free speech and open debate. It can lead to environments where dissenting opinions are labeled as offensive, discouraging dialogue and limiting intellectual diversity.

Moreover, it can be exploited for political gain. Politicians might use identity politics to pander to specific groups, resulting in superficial gestures rather than meaningful change, undermining trust in political institutions. We see this with both sides of the political spectrum.

Identity politics, while aiming to empower marginalized groups and address systemic inequalities, can also have several negative consequences. Key among these are the promotion of groupthink, the reinforcement of stereotypes, and the increase of societal divisiveness.

## Promotion of Groupthink

One such consequence is the promotion of groupthink, where the pressure to conform to the prevailing views within a group can stifle healthy debate and critical thinking. This suppression of dissent can limit the group's ability to address complex issues effectively, as innovative solutions and diverse perspectives are often overlooked. Moreover, identity politics can create echo chambers where members are only exposed to ideas that reinforce their existing beliefs, further entrenching those beliefs and reducing exposure to a broader range of viewpoints.

## Reinforcement of Stereotypes

Another significant downside is the reinforcement of stereotypes. Identity politics can lead to the homogenization of group members, promoting the perception that all individuals within a particular identity group share the same views, experiences, and needs. This can marginalize subgroups and individuals whose experiences differ from the dominant narrative. Additionally, emphasizing certain aspects of identity, such as victimhood, can inadvertently reinforce negative stereotypes, portraying groups as inherently weak or oppressed rather than recognizing their agency and resilience. This oversimplification can result in inaccurate narratives that fail to capture the nuanced and intersectional nature of individual experiences.

## Increase of Societal Divisiveness

Furthermore, identity politics can increase societal divisiveness by emphasizing differences rather than commonalities. This polarization fosters an "us vs. them" mentality, making compromise and mutual understanding more difficult. By focusing on specific identity groups, there is a risk of fragmenting society into isolated segments, each advocating for its own interests, which can undermine social cohesion and the sense of a shared community. The framing of issues in terms of group identity rather than individual viewpoints can also escalate conflicts, heightening tensions both between and within different identity groups.

## Reflection on America's Identity

Next, we will be taking a step back to reflect on America's identity. This allows us to appreciate the complex interplay of unity and diversity that has defined the nation. The original form of identity politics, rooted in the founding principles and early struggles of the United States, fostered a nation built on the ideals of liberty, diversity, and innovation. These values have shaped the country's development and continue to influence its trajectory.

# Part 3 - The Role of Identity Politics in America's Formation

The impact and importance of identity politics, both positive and negative, are undeniable. To better understand this concept, it is helpful to examine America's national identity, which can be seen as an early form of identity politics. By exploring the foundations of American identity, we can gain insight into the values and dynamics it has fostered within our nation.

America's identity has been shaped by a variety of factors, including its founding principles, diverse population, and the continuous struggle for civil rights and equality. From its inception, the United States was built on the ideals of liberty, individualism, and democracy. These principles were enshrined in foundational documents like the Declaration of Independence and the Constitution, which emphasized the importance of personal freedom and the protection of individual rights.

In a way, the early development of American identity can be viewed as a precursor to modern identity politics. The formation of the United States involved various groups advocating for their interests and rights, such as the colonists seeking independence from British rule and the framers of the Constitution negotiating the balance of power among states. This process of negotiating and asserting different identities and interests laid the groundwork for the nation's democratic ethos.

The early struggles and negotiations that shaped American identity fostered several key values within the nation:

1. **Liberty and Individual Rights:** The fight for independence and the establishment of a democratic government underscored the importance of personal freedom and the protection of individual rights. This emphasis on liberty has been a defining characteristic of American identity and continues to influence the nation's political and social landscape.
2. **Diversity and Pluralism:** America's identity has always been marked by its diversity. The nation has been a melting pot of cultures, ethnicities, and religions, leading to a rich tapestry of experiences and perspectives. This diversity has fostered a spirit of pluralism, where different groups coexist and contribute to the nation's growth.
3. **Innovation and Progress:** The emphasis on individualism and freedom has also driven a culture of innovation and progress. Americans have been encouraged to think independently, challenge existing norms, and pursue new ideas. This spirit of innovation has led to numerous technological, scientific, and cultural advancements that have shaped the modern world.

## Impact on Modern Identity Politics

Modern identity politics continues this legacy by advocating for the rights and recognition of marginalized groups. It seeks to address systemic inequalities and ensure that diverse voices are heard and represented. While this advocacy has led to significant social progress, it has also sparked debates about the potential for divisiveness and the risk of prioritizing group identities over shared national values.

At the heart of American democracy is the principle of individual liberty, which includes the freedom to think and express oneself independently. The Founding Fathers emphasized this in the Constitution and the Bill of Rights, particularly through the First Amendment, which guarantees freedom of speech, press, and assembly. These rights ensure that citizens can voice their opinions, challenge government policies, and advocate for change without fear of reprisal. Independent thought thus underpins democratic participation, allowing for a marketplace of ideas where diverse perspectives can be considered and debated. This diversity of thought is crucial for informed decision-making and effective governance, as it prevents the dominance of any single ideology or group. Next, we take at look at this diversity of thought or independent thought.

# Part 4 - Independent Thought and Freedom

Foundations of Independent Thought

The foundations of independent thought in the United States stem from a blend of Enlightenment philosophy, revolutionary principles, constitutional guarantees, and a commitment to education, all within a diverse cultural context.

The American Revolution exemplified and furthered independent thought. Works like Thomas Paine's "Common Sense" and the Declaration of Independence championed self-governance and individual rights. The Declaration, in particular, asserted the people's right to change or abolish oppressive governments, embedding the principle of independent thought in the nation's ethos.

The U.S. Constitution institutionalized independent thought through its system of checks and balances, separation of powers, and the Bill of Rights, which protect freedoms such as speech, press, and assembly. These structures prevent the monopolization of power and encourage diverse opinions and critical discourse.

Education and democratic participation are crucial in fostering independent thought. Early American leaders like Thomas Jefferson advocated for public education to cultivate an informed and critical citizenry. Public schooling has since become a means to promote inquiry and debate.

America's cultural diversity further supports independent thought by encouraging the exchange of multiple perspectives. This pluralism fosters an environment where individuals are prompted to critically evaluate their beliefs and consider alternative viewpoints.

American identity is closely linked to a spirit of innovation and entrepreneurship, both of which rely heavily on independent thought. The ability to think creatively and challenge existing paradigms has driven countless technological, scientific, and cultural advancements. From Thomas Edison to Steve Jobs, American inventors and entrepreneurs have transformed the world through their innovative ideas and independent thinking. This culture of innovation is nurtured by educational institutions that encourage critical thinking and problem-solving, preparing individuals to contribute meaningfully to society. Independent thought fosters an environment where questioning the status quo is not only accepted but celebrated, leading to breakthroughs that propel society forward.

## Freedom of Thought

Independent thought should be celebrated, not chastised, as it is fundamental to our nation's history. The freedoms we enjoy today were hard-fought and earned through the courage and critical thinking of our predecessors. From the Enlightenment ideas that inspired the Founding Fathers to the revolutionary struggle for self-governance, the United States has always valued individual liberty and critical discourse. Our constitutional protections and democratic principles are designed to nurture and safeguard independent thought, making it a cornerstone of American identity and progress.

Independent thought is a safeguard against conformity and authoritarianism. In a society where conformity is enforced, creativity, progress, and personal freedom are stifled. The American emphasis on individuality ensures that people are free to pursue their own paths, make their own decisions, and develop their own beliefs. This resistance to conformity is evident in various social movements throughout American history, from the civil rights movement to the women's suffrage movement, where individuals and groups have stood up against prevailing norms to advocate for justice and equality. Independent thought empowers people to question unjust practices and policies, fostering a culture of resilience and resistance against oppression.

## Enabler of Personal Growth

On a personal level, independent thought is essential for self-actualization and growth. It allows individuals to form their own identities, make informed choices, and take responsibility for their actions. This sense of agency is a fundamental aspect of the American dream, where individuals are encouraged to pursue their passions and aspirations. The freedom to think independently cultivates a sense of empowerment and self-worth, enabling people to navigate life's challenges with confidence and integrity.

## Promoter of Social Progress

Independent thought also promotes social progress by encouraging empathy and understanding across diverse communities. When individuals are free to explore different perspectives and ideas, they are more likely to develop a deeper appreciation for the experiences and viewpoints of others. This openness can lead to greater social cohesion and the ability to address complex social issues in a more nuanced and effective manner. In a multicultural society like the United States, the ability to think independently and critically is vital for fostering inclusivity and mutual respect.

Next we dive a little deeper and reflect. Having thoroughly explored the foundations of independent thought, we can now examine how it intersects with identity politics. This requires understanding how individual cognitive freedom interacts with collective social identities. By exploring this intersection, we can uncover the dynamic relationship between personal intellectual autonomy and the frameworks of identity politics. This analysis will reveal both the conflicts and collaborations that occur when independent thinking meets the communal and often rigid aspects of identity-based affiliations.

# Part 5 - Are Identity Politics a threat to Independent thought?

## Reflecting and Summarizing

Identity politics, the practice of organizing around social identities such as race, gender, sexuality, and religion to achieve political ends, can pose a threat to independent thought. While it aims to address historical injustices and give voice to marginalized groups, its focus on group identity over individual perspectives can stifle critical thinking and open discourse.

## Homogenization of Thought

One of the main ways identity politics threatens independent thought is through the homogenization of opinion within identity groups. By prioritizing group identity, individuals may feel pressured to conform to the dominant views within their group, fearing ostracism or backlash for expressing dissenting opinions. This can suppress diverse viewpoints and discourage critical examination of issues, as the validity of an argument is often judged based on the speaker's identity rather than the content of their ideas.

## Polarization and Tribalism

Identity politics can also exacerbate societal polarization and tribalism. By categorizing individuals primarily by their social identities, it creates an "us versus them" mentality. This divisiveness fosters an environment where people are more likely to reject ideas from outside their group without due consideration, undermining the possibility of genuine dialogue and mutual understanding. Such polarization makes it difficult for individuals to engage with opposing viewpoints thoughtfully, reducing opportunities for independent thought.

## Victimhood Culture

Another aspect of identity politics that threatens independent thought is the promotion of a victimhood culture. When political discourse centers around perceived grievances and victimization, it can lead individuals to adopt a mindset that prioritizes their identity-based experiences of oppression over objective analysis and critical thinking. This focus on victimhood can discourage personal agency and self-reflection, as individuals are taught to see their challenges primarily through the lens of identity-based oppression rather than exploring a wider array of personal and societal factors.

## Censorship and Cancel Culture

Identity politics can also lead to censorship and the rise of "cancel culture" where individuals or ideas that do not align with the dominant narrative of a particular identity group are silenced or ostracized. This culture of censorship inhibits free speech and open debate, essential components of independent thought. When people fear retribution for expressing controversial or unpopular opinions, they are less likely to engage in the kind of critical thinking and open dialogue that fosters independent thought.

## What now? Where do we go from here?

While identity politics seeks to address genuine social inequalities, its emphasis on group identity over individual thought can undermine the principles of independent thought. By promoting conformity within groups, exacerbating polarization, fostering a victimhood mentality, and encouraging censorship, identity politics can stifle the open discourse and critical thinking that are essential for a healthy democratic society. To preserve independent thought, it is crucial to balance the recognition of group identities with a commitment to individual autonomy and open, respectful dialogue.

These conclusions vividly illustrate my experience during the social media encounter I mentioned in the introduction. There is now context to begin to answer some of the questions I posed in the introduction:

- "Can we communicate without yelling at one another?"

- "Why is everyone so triggered by things?"
- "Why can't a person from both sides have a discussion of understanding like my grandfather and I used to have?"
- "Why are people labeling whole groups of people as racists, socialists, snowflakes, neocons, libtards, fascists, and many others?"

That encounter was a turning point, my personal "aha" moment, where abstract ideas about independent thought and identity became tangible realities.

We can see how easily we can fall into things like stereotyping, even in digital spaces, and how crucial it is to maintain our individuality and critical thinking. This moment underscored the importance of balancing our identities with the ability to think independently. It taught me to value diverse perspectives while holding onto my unique viewpoints.

Reflecting on this, I understand that maintaining this balance is key to personal growth and meaningful dialogue. This experience has fundamentally shaped my approach to discussions, both online and offline, emphasizing the importance of independent thought in navigating complex social landscapes.

# Conclusion - Identity politics and Independent thought can co-exist!

Yes, individuals can have independent thoughts while maintaining their identity. Independent thought and identity are not mutually exclusive; rather, they can coexist in a way that enriches both personal and communal experiences.

Independent thought and maintaining one's identity can complement each other, forming a powerful foundation for personal freedom and societal progress. By embracing the complexity of their identity, engaging with diverse opinions, balancing autonomy with identity, and resisting societal pressures, individuals can think independently while remaining true to their backgrounds and experiences. This interplay not only enriches personal intellectual development but also contributes to a more inclusive and thoughtful society.

## Embracing Complexity

Understanding and valuing one's identity provide a unique perspective that enhances independent thinking. Personal experiences and cultural backgrounds inform viewpoints, allowing individuals to approach problems and ideas with a richer, more nuanced understanding. For instance, a person's racial, gender, or cultural identity can offer insights into social issues that might be overlooked by others. Recognizing the complexity of identity involves acknowledging how it shapes our perceptions while also questioning how these perceptions influence our thinking.

## Engaging with Diverse Opinions

Independent thought thrives in environments that encourage open dialogue and the exchange of diverse opinions. Engaging with various perspectives, both within and outside one's identity group, helps individuals refine their ideas and challenge assumptions. This intellectual diversity fosters critical thinking and innovation. Open dialogue requires intellectual courage—being willing to question and even disagree with the dominant views within one's identity group. This process of engagement and reflection leads to more robust and original thinking.

## Balancing Identity and Autonomy

While identity shapes experiences and perspectives, individuals possess the agency to think autonomously. Maintaining one's identity while thinking independently involves a delicate balance of respecting one's background and asserting the freedom to form personal opinions. This balance is crucial for fostering independent thought. Self-expression plays a key role here; maintaining one's identity should not mean conforming to all group norms or expectations. Encouraging self-expression within identity groups leads to a richer, more diverse set of ideas and innovations.

## Resisting Societal Pressures

Societal pressures and group dynamics can sometimes stifle independent thought. It is essential to be mindful of these influences and strive to think critically and independently, even when it means going against the grain of one's identity group. This resistance to conformity is a form of exercising personal freedom. Creating environments that celebrate both identity and independent thought is essential. Educational institutions, workplaces, and communities that value diversity and encourage critical thinking can help individuals navigate the interplay between their identity and independent thought.

## The Theme of Freedom

At its core, the ability to think independently while maintaining one's identity is a profound expression of freedom. It represents the liberty to explore diverse perspectives, challenge prevailing norms, and articulate unique viewpoints. This freedom is not only personal but also societal. A society that values independent thought alongside respect for individual identities is more likely to foster innovation, inclusivity, and progress. Such a society benefits from the collective wisdom of its diverse members, each contributing their distinct insights and ideas.

## Conclusion

In conclusion, the interplay between independent thought and identity is fundamental to personal freedom and societal advancement. By embracing the complexity of identity, engaging with diverse opinions, balancing autonomy with identity, and resisting societal pressures, individuals can cultivate independent thought while honoring their backgrounds and experiences. This dynamic enriches personal intellectual development and fosters a more inclusive, thoughtful, and free society.

# Resources

identity politics. (2024). In *Merriam-Webster Dictionary.* https://www.merriam-webster.com/dictionary/identity%20politics

*Identity Politics (Stanford Encyclopedia of Philosophy).* (2020, July 11). https://plato.stanford.edu/entries/identity-politics/#RefeCite

Chandler, D., & Munday, R. (2011). A Dictionary of Media and Communication. In *Oxford University Press eBooks.* https://doi.org/10.1093/acref/9780199568758.001.0001

Crenshaw, K. (1989). Demarginalizing the Intersection of Race and Sex: A Black Feminist Critique of Antidiscrimination Doctrine, Feminist Theory, and Antiracist Politics. *University of Chicago Legal Forum*, 1989(1), 139-167.

Taylor, K.-Y. (2017). *How We Get Free: Black Feminism and the Combahee River Collective.* Haymarket Books.

www.ingramcontent.com/pod-product-compliance
Lightning Source LLC
Chambersburg PA
CBHW051900250726

48659CB00006B/2323